key and other poems

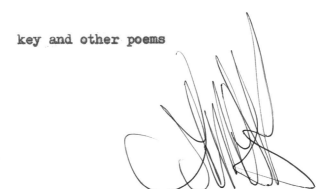

layerjam

Every page in Key was designed by hand then scanned at high resolution for lithographic print. The words were hand-typed and hand-formatted by the author using an Olympia Carina 2 typewriter. The illustrations are fineliner with acrylic and watercolour paint, originally made on Arches Aquarelle paper, and printed here on paper certified as sustainable by the Forestry Stewardship Council. This print run was certified as carbon neutral by Preferred by Nature. The logos that confirm Key's sustainability, to be found on the next page, are the only elements of digital design in this book.

Key and Other Poems

Key, the title poem of this collection, is now a film starring
T. S. Eliot Prize winner Joelle Taylor.

"In their intricate simplicities these poems come from deep
in the human mind and out of the shadows. When scientists
send rockets into far-away space to introduce themselves
they include the latest pop music and snippets of trivial TV.
Instead they should send a copy of these poems."
Edward Bond

James E. Kenward performs his poetry accompanied by concert
pianist Bota Zakir, as one half of Beezy and The Breeze.
Key is also the name of an album of poems selected from this
book and spoken in arrangement with timeless piano classics.
James gives his voice to number one ranking productions
on Audible, and directs films inspired by his poetry.
Other poems in this book are songs.

"I hope he keeps putting his immense talents to such effective use."
Time Out Critic's Choice

"Kenward shines bright and is destined for a great future."
The Stage

Information about the recorded music, film, concerts and artworks
that stem from these words is available on the Layerjam website.

www.layerjam.com

Layerjam

Key and Other Poems

www.layerjam.com

Art scans made by Barry Pollitt and Becky Terry at
Pollittbureau Art Print Ltd, Christchurch, England.
Illustrations Copyright 2024 by Leia Lorelai

Cover design by Jonathan Ashmore and James E. Kenward
Cover illustrations by Leia Lorelai
Colourist: Suvi Karjalainen

Printed on FSC certified paper by FINIDR s.r.o.
Czeski Cieszyn, Czech Republic

Layerjam
Munich office
Waltherstrasse 11, 80337 Munich, Germany

James E. Kenward selbst. schriftstellr.
145/119/91340

James E. Kenward

Key and Other Poems

Illustrated by Leia Lorelai

A tree will be planted the autumn after Key is printed so as to account directly for the paper used in the printing of the book. A Heidleberg Speedmaster XL – 106 was used to print Key. Heidleberg are pioneers in the combination of carbon-neutral projects with efficiency in modern printing techniques: by means of a climate protection project implemented in Togo, West Africa, the company supports forestation of an untouched region which is exposed to erosion and desertification. In practice the forestation process means that a mixed forest consisting of pure, native, woody species will be planted in a protected area of 1000 hectares. This will help establish an autoregulatory ecosystem. Layerjam are glad to be part of efforts to make beautiful, sustainable books.

Thank you, Alex, for being an endless source of inspiration.

contents.

soon

new

for the earth

soon

key

the bucket lowered slowly down - the key within;
the king above, full-crowned in imperial modesty.

the small child looked around, grabbed the key
and ran
unwavering
the clown had seized the now
and praised herself
unprecedented, feverous, nervous
full-tilt, off-ski -

forgetting the princessly she
held golden and bejewelléd key
that fit the lock
within the king
behind her
thief
that jack the lad
who sparkled as she ran -

growing tomatoes

"come and get some of this
soil i've made," she says -
"it's good stuff."

layered the leaf
to make the mulch -
dark, chocolate, fibrous
crumble juice
- tomato drink

they'll suck on that stuff
'til they're ripe enough for
rinsing in the kitchen sink

those toms'll take all the pain away
from those tired joints - they will -
and she'll slice 'em;
ask me make a dressing;
not needed for what's
from her garden - growth
richer than finest virgin oil
- i have a mum makes soil
so grab a shovel, grateful
to turn life's lustre
and death's spoils.

thank you mother -
thank you mother -
for your toils.

firestarter
for robin

the sadness of it stretches me
as i had thought it couldn't quite
to see a luminescence be
and then too early dimmed, the light.
the pain, the artist's hand, but why
that sharing heart is rare to bright
yet can flare out and fill the sky?
for us - sky blue that grew from night.
the living state is ill-embraced
by some with gifts to give us life;
is it a blessing we are graced
with soul by those with no respite?
so grateful i, yet so i hate,
that those share best that suffocate.

wax

candles like us
burn strong then not at all.
the brighter the fire
the quicker the brawl
of wick and wax
to molten stall
and bottle's bottom
after fall -

quand on est dans la merde jusqu'au cou...
or.
if the hat fits

1.
did you keep it?
i know you kept it.
would you please look after it?
i don't want to worry.
i mean, i'm pretty sure you must have picked it up.
it's my fault for paying attention
when that man in those stories
stashes the valuables under his.

2.
i don't know why this is happening -
but i'm in a hatters, back of piccadilly circus,
buying the hat i'm going to wear
when i meet you out there.
this one is the hat.
i can tell, if only by the price i'm prepared to pay.

3.
if you didn't pick it up maybe mother georgia did.
i hope she did.
below her bread basket and sword you began to run,
then, above tbilisi you flew.
knocked my hat clean off.
if mother georgia has it
i reckon she'll guard and nourish it
but i reckon you've got it.
will you?

4.
i still wear the hat.
think of the joy when your legs hit my waist
and the hat hit the dust.
thud.

5.
it is later.
you are very far.
i must have intended
you to have something valuable of mine
— to make you a present of me.
that or i scented danger and thought i should
put it in a safe place.
either way — only just now, sitting on this pavement
in marseilles, sipping memories of you
that are as new as beaujolais,
i remember how, before we met that day,
something possessed me to
put my heart in my hat.

mop
for costin

he stands in the doorway
with his big dopey eyes,
this friend of mine who
likes to sleep outside
but pops over when the
weather turns, on winter nights.

"you know that woman
jumped from the flats?"
i nod. "so much blood -
no one would clean it
after the ambulance
picked the body up -
so i did. a crowd watched."
his voice resonates
but sometimes
the resonance cuts off.

he splashes a flood
from the bath. i put his
clothes on for a wash
and consider the people
who cut the mental health
services as i screw the
head onto the mop.

ambrosia

jonny you are neither short nor tall
but somewhere in the middle -
nowadays you are probably none of these at all
as in hospital the custom is horizontal.

jonny you are neither brunette nor blonde,
but a silver fox - in fact are you bald?

jonny i thought that by now you'd be dead
but you have a good heart and good head, it is said;
i have seen these things so attest they're correct;
they're well-illustrated by the deep love you get
from visiting types like sarah henley bennett
and people like me, who are miles away,
writing poetry consisting of things not to say -

jon, i don't know what the deal is for you;
whether you're sprightly or riddled with tubes;
but i thought just maybe it was one of them ones;
you know - "let's just take every day as it comes..."

since tomorrow is never so far away
i thought that i had better say, today
- i think of you dearly, a diamond indeed,
big love, drink ambrosia for me, and godspeed -

clouds

an old man in the boozer
(used to run the tank museum)
tells me. seven out of ten men
having been asked to use their
rifles liberally in world war two,
shot at clouds regularly - surmising
them to be as good a bullet bury
as any. clouds catch water from
the seas, why not a shell too?
the orders, regarding expected
targets, struck the soldiers
to be as sensible as the skies
were clear, back home, here
in england. the clarity of the skies
are doubtful too, in northern france -
germany also (whose men must
have been doing the same since
the other side won, in spite of said
evaporative aim). perhaps all men know,
from wherever they hail, that bullets
must be caught - and clouds are good
at catching. were a man's soul clear
as unblemished skies, a bullet
might pass through or fly straight by.
but man's soul is cloud blemished,
even as he tries. shoot the skies,
the skies live. shoot a man and he dies.

```
        ecstasy
        for leo


    ecstasy - blindfolded truly
    seeing colours dancing
    outstretch so far as to soar
    hopeful, anguished, shining
    lip first through all the many
    layers of now - arch, 'ey -

    bridge and plummet
    light crackling into the chasm
    where joy and sorrow meet -
    invigorate, burst, glow
    ripple and drown
    ripple and drown

    shatter, scatter you
    then shake hands again
    with you my friend -
    perhaps the blemishes
    will dart off like so many
    bait fish in between you
    as you part you and plunge
    into the river in the chasm
    where joy and sorrow meet

    shake hands with you again
    a little more you maybe
    and swim, lip first
    kiss it all - and be it
```

as the bait fish burst
away upstream, and
dive themselves to feed the lake
beneath that feeds the stream
like so many poisonous seeds
these little fish transform and breath
to peacock feathers, now the colours
of the torrent that you run

as you swim, 'ey
guided by the love that you've become
you are all and all is one
as you swim, 'ey
flicker, scatter
sing, 'ey
out to sea

hanzel

i tried to hide the legs behind black sacks on the street,
next to the seat, struts, and the chair's back piece.

you saw dents in the laminate and asked
why i had done it; "son" i replied, "i was drunk."
which is a bad answer, but better than the other;

"because i wanted something i couldn't have."
that would be setting a bad example. i am not a child so
make choices; son, i love her, but she can't love us as one.

son, i've chosen, the chair is broken, she is gone.

crow

there's a riddle of grey roads i know;
i know them very well -
they're full of life these roads,
and now these roads are hell -
you make your own though;
so they say - it's here for me;
a feeling we are feeding
on the garden of the world -
thank god that there is sometimes
sun, sometimes a pearl chewed
from the coal, i can stand up
sometimes, crows shine blue;
in blackness they can glow;
i'm reaching for the mother
'cause i know she isn't well -
i'm surrounded by desire;
this town's a death of things to sell;
you can taste it in the fiver
melted in my beer's smell;
if my liver stops tomorrow then
i won't be there to tell you
that i still see light peck peck-
ing inside every darkened hole.

```
            fall
          for lisa


on the way to the shelter
for women who have it shit
she hits the ground

skinny as a snake in a pit
making a puddle with a head nick
an inch thicker than her shivering lips

i'm okay, she says;
i'm used to it,
but, she says

as she bleeds blood dry as sand
from her shrunken head
into the palm of my hand;

i just got out of hospital.
tonight's my first night
in my own bed -
back in the shelter.

i reassure her, it's a small cut,
as we lie in the gutter together
and she works her limp legs to
straighten, rather than open,
```

and the red spreads puddle brown
i comfort her; the helpful passer -
fixed smile like some sort of happy
good luck clown; it's okay love

- this fall was not enough -
you will be getting up;
there will be more
falling before
staying down.

                    all

        it doesn't matter how you die -
        from whence your name is called;
        if a bullet has it 'graved upon;
        or you're asleep so cannot fall

        you'll end up flower shaped;
        in starry space; and in the soil
        - all of the above, and more;
        yes friend - you'll be it all

        this body will be ocean
        this body will be trees
        this body will be ghosts
        and this body's you and me

little things

some things are best
not said with words;
it takes a whisper
of an inkling of a curve;
it takes a kiss of an
imagining, the salt of
sea, the loss of shame,
the reimagining of sin;
the gain of she and they
and him combined in
many ways, the aim of
love when lone - the breath
that does not try to win -
the freedom in the little things
and pleasure ever nourishing.

new

change

her hair's like the dark
in the dips of the bark
and her eyes are
the growth of the earth.

her lips are the kiss
that shape everyone's wish,
and her white teeth
are rooted in mirth.

her tongue tastes of yes;
and her words do not guess;
and her throat's never burred
by a curse.

her breasts are as round
as a whale song is loud -
and her down
is as soft as her purse.

i say to her; "honey - sweet sugar, o nectar;
when you're with me you won't feel no pain."
"darling," she says, "you know that ain't true.
i love you, and love ain't that way."

her hands are as small
as a buttercup ball
flower dancing
first morning of may.

her belly will call you
to legs, i must warn you —
as long as
a long summer's day.

her heart is the start
— though it can't change the past
it turns sorrow to joy
now, today.

come and rejoice with her;
come give your tears
to be scattered
as wide as the rain

which quenches the thirst
of all broken, or worse,
and grows it
anew once again.

i say to her; "honey - sweet sugar, o nectar;
when i'm with you i won't feel no pain - "
"darling," she says, "you know that ain't true -
you love me, and love ain't that way."

take caution my friend;
what is started can't end
and there's nothing
that hurts worse than change.

she will spin into beauty
as wide as her booty
one buttercup
filled with your pain -

if you offer it up,
then for each buttercup
she will change you
again, and again.

barnacles

life is a cliff face
covered in barnacles
climbed butt naked

bloody rough cliff face
ouch

friends are the holds
oops
sorry mate
didn't mean to -

thanks

sharing

a problem shared
is a problem halved.
we are together while we read this;
let's chop our loneliness to pieces
and watch it flutter past.

fennel

little pieces of fennel -
sallow, now come summer, green;
i've been drifting to you,
red;
green grows longer in between.

i have to take a watch
from off my wrist these days
to dance a skein of skin

i want it pure, i want it clean

my body
is a chequerboard
of all the lives
i've been

i would have murdered for you, red,
but i'm murdering the murderers for you, green

talking to tomatoes

the plant smells better than the fruits
and the fruits smell like health itself;
it's too soon for their wealth.

o - the green; the nose between the leaves -
let's reach for the sun above
let's smell of earth and love.

truth

washed up as old socks
limp cocks and ink spots
her lot laugh a lot
the laughter's clean
i feel hot

the sun swells
the fan died
it's holiday time
been with the same girl
fifty eight weeks on the trot

she asks nothing of me
but i slowly build all
so she will make me
want to kill-fuck her
like any good mother-whore

don't know much about loving.
i watch her sleeping; she knows
there's more than this;
i'll hear her truth more.

god goes
for moe

he's scratching a nipple
beneath a filthy suit jacket loose as a duvet cover,
purple lining still bright
as grease matting his hair.
his beard is treacherous, foul, honest somehow.

i can smell him from here.
a rumpled stack of something old, standing, leaking.

the rivulet lengthens
out along the pavement's edge
refusing to enter the gutter.
behind the beard
the pisser's easy ecstasy is as understated
as the waterfall from the top of the too big left shoe below him
that nobody notices.

this piss goes on for days.
he is five feet away.

i am benched on the edge of a forgetting place.

i sip my pint and wait
for the piss to pass five, six, seven, eight,
ten, fifteen paving slabs.
there is another man sitting next to me, carefully dressed,
square faced. i point out our proximity to miracles.
the man opens his eyes enough to notice –
then spreads word in haste.

mouths fall open above cocktails
right close to the beginning of a fantastic urine trail.
when the ever lengthening river reaches the next block
its rumpled source looks at us, speaks, then repeats.

the man sitting down next to me,
who looks like the man sitting down next to him,
which is like a corporation carefully disguised as an artist,
listens to the pissers words and asks
- why does he keep saying: this is not my fault

- he's not saying that, i point out,
as i ponder the theme of guilt built
onto the lips of my neighbour's mouth.

the pisser looks at us and speaks again.
his voice has a timbre old as rain.

- i give you my water.

paula, who i've seen around,
her eyes as open and closed as a fan
mentions something about a bank i think
or financial services, or marketing, or something.

the bright pink of paula's top is momentarily balanced by the drab
rags of another crumpled passer. a lady with kind eyes in a raisin
face crack shrivelled atop the physicality of a crutch.
i know this lady and, pleased she's not dead yet, give her a hug.

paula's eyes suddenly fan open. she sees the river's source.
an inadvertent comment parts her face;
words with the honesty of a well-needed piss
passing penis lips issue forth. paula says
- i could never be brave enough to do something like that.
she quickly tenses to stop the flow, knowing disgust
according to a set of rules undiscussed is best,
of course. her eyes fan shut.

- i give you my water.

this piss grows spectacular.
frothing yellow hell.
buildings begin to go.
in the city, down the road,
towers cascade as easily as the pisser's jacket crumples.

dirty, filthy, rich, miracles.
this piss is simple as brown slugs humping in the rain.

his eyes are the entrance to coal mines,
dead souls dare us from the black.

enormity of river delivered, quite relaxed
dragging a one-wheeled suitcase from which sticks
an almost empty bottle of frosty jacks
that i wish were real scrumpy but is about as cider as
the creatives in the bar are creative,
full-stenched, marked, but unnoticed,
limping, a little, down the road
god goes.

defense services technological academy
    pyin oo lwin, myanmar

how do they teach them
to walk like that?
it goes; left-right-left.

a flicker of a smile
on a fat teenaged face;
mostly i smell death.

camouflage in the shops
that we pass by
suggests no second guess -

there's an air of that truth
that says peaceful
is killing so as to protect.

. . . .

yet our table is served
by flower-shirted boys,
guitars hanging on walls
by their necks.

i journey through kitchens
seeing life, alive-living,
full flavours and sweat -
no regrets.

. . . .

outside of the town
is a monument round;
giant warriors stand
for respect.

they're tall as a hall,
curved swords poised to fall -
they're like manga
cartoon robo-tec

a cross between
samurai giants and
pedigree kill
kill and kill s.a.s

school boys below
from school gates march to lunch
and they really don't know
much as yet

and i breath in the brass;
the left-rights as they pass;
i'm afraid of what
happens next.

                    the weight
             for naoise with thanks

the plate opposite could fill up
with one long tendrilous vomit
of hurt.
          the ache that comes naturally
thickened with that inflicted on others by me.
this latter comes naturally too sometimes.
this latter puts the chunk in queasy.
the person sitting opposite me says:

"you look tired daddy.
i want to show you something.
can i show you something daddy, please?"

earlier that day
we'd found an object in the sand by the see-saw.

small and curved. it weighs.

round it silver strips outline two slender sets of hips
that bulge from black metal ore.
something earth, something human,
something smooth, something raw.

"show me - " i say.

he's seen the spark's gone from my gaze
even though i've pulled a bright blue ribbon
from his ear 'cause it was scrunched up in his brain -
his laughter eases it out, and stops me

sneezing clods of pain, though i almost lose an eye;
"ribbons are fine - but no sticks at table - " i explain.

he tells me he knows what the strange weight is for.
he says he knows exactly.
i've never seen anything like it before.

so we chop our bangers into mashy holes
slather them in gravy, and then oven them a mo' -
he has to show me something,
and there's a chance the toads may grow.

"help me tie this knot here, daddy."
i tie another there -

and with a gentle flick of the wrist
the weight circumnavigates the stick's tip
then the ribbon spiral fits the stick
as close as ocean fits a ship

"back the other way!"
weight up and off, aloft
then gently down the ribbon lays -
a little impetus for beauty
may unmuddle any maze;
the weight swings back, the ribbon flies
my son says, "let's do this for days!"
"the toads are tasty, eat 'em up
because it's time for bed - " i say.

"ssh, close your eyes."
"but where's the thing, daddy? the thing!"
"can i borrow it? for the evening?"
"yes, daddy."
"sweet dreaming."

he kips. sweet asleep. soft breathing.

i put the kettle on and sit.

i'm going to unwind this weight slowly for a bit.

hard to know what to make of it.
the weight.
new and very old.

the fire filled earth wrapped close by a cold blue strip.

coughing up phlegm ain't nice
but it can be fun to spit.

sometimes the weight of sadness flies.

daddy, it's for this.

grow

it is gentle, sweet and will grow.
settle winter's first fall of snow;
flowers come after, bursting
white then yellow, small and bright
- and green, lush green; the world
begins to grow

so bountiful
so beautiful, so whole;
a never-ending turn of lustre
and the other fuels the soul.

it is gentle, sweet and will grow.
a babe's unwrinkling skin;
steady the legs upon the foal;
you make me without sin
and alight when i was coal.

it is gentle, sweet - and will grow -
this love, love, is as certain as
the turning of the world and
in my heart it dances, love,
and in my heart it glows.

bright joy in small things

she finds
bright joy
in small things

she says
'oh, i like that'
with emphasis
like a wet kiss
about nothing
in particular

those who find
the amazing
quickly

live well

stay with them

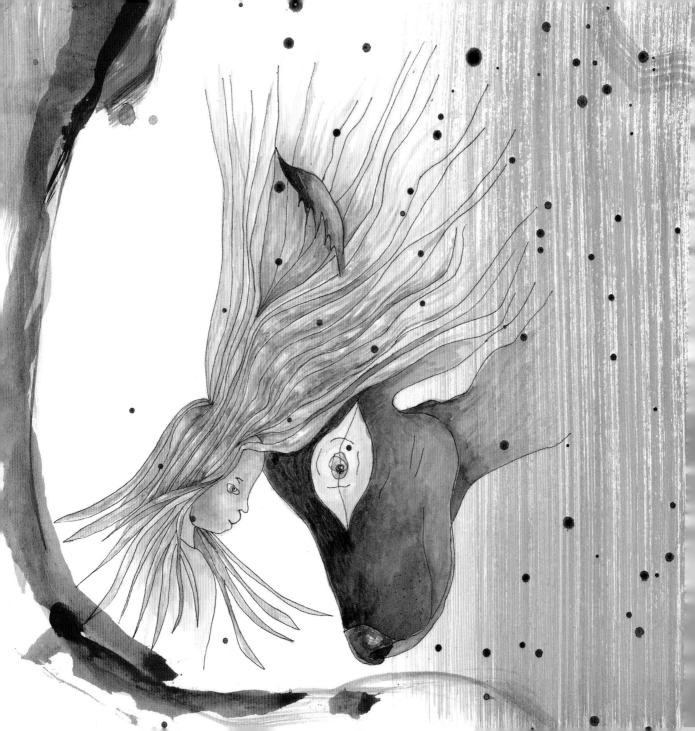

dog

he bonds our family and builds structure
strong as the pyramids; through old laws
deep and holy he pulls the pack together.
sacrifice is made, and labour without pause
slowly becomes light as air; his hair snows
through our home like the scatter of thoughts
in a head - one body's mess brings patience
and togetherness; you must just take a breath.
simplicity in pure attention guides him;
days begin with kind eyes and a rested chin
- he gives like the sun and runs like the wind
filling moments with joy and with learning.

bliss

love ain't bliss
it's bliss sometimes
in work and
stormy weather

an easy life is
all very fine
but some bliss
is better than never

flaws

if you do not embrace others
with all their flaws
you will never help them
nor understand yours

tears

when those big tears
drop from those big eyes
mummy, little mummy, big mummy,
the biggest tears you've ever seen mummy -
i know your heart cries.

don't try too hard to stem those tears mummy;
it's natural, mummy, melancholy;
you gotta take it in your stride.
you'd do anything to stop the sadness,
fill that boy with joy and gladness;
you'd break up worlds with wrath,
those worlds their madness not,
and naught their suffering to subside.

so lovely, mummy, don't get anxious
although those falling tears are roundest
ocean blue, and sighs the saddest,
kindest mummy, don't get savage;
let your heart be by love ravaged
free. hearts once one cannot attached be.
nine months no tears then streams for years;
you see there ain't no cure for sadness
however hard you try for he.

it comes to all, it comes to every
no one can pluck another's plenty
'cause more of it is ever ready

no don't get mad and don't get heavy;
be light amongst that melancholy;
let's all be sad and all be happy
supporting each and everybody -

don't drown in tears, don't stop their flow;
we won't be angry building boats
'neath skies of joy on sorrow-moats
from castles-calm to lands of hope
we mustn't let love smother notes
of what comes naturally to most.

look at this gig - the gig's a goat;
it's slippery as a bar of soap;
so high it climbs and low it mopes;
let's stroke the ears and plait the throat.

so come on, mummy, don't be funny;
you and me, we're in this boat;
no one's to blame when it ain't sunny -
loose that rain man from that choke,
then suck on lemon, and spoon down honey,
and trust in tears, and on them float.

halloween

10 and a half years ago
i became your father.
(you no longer haggle
over the extra half years
in between). it's corona -

this year was the first
without you on halloween -

leia had a bit of a cough.

three years ago she saw
me make ogre fingers with
mini cucumbers; and ghoul's
eyes with grapes and raisins,
before i sewed the collar for your
dracula; it was a good occasion.

this year we received your
costume by photo on whatsapp.

the head on a plate was great -
almost as good as last year
when we first created the look;
at least you got the make-up
through in the post

                     - and anyway
i suppose me and your mum mostly
used to argue when doing trick or treat
about the size of the sweet stash -
or was it about the sweets?

i wish i could have been
with you for a bit.

                     those pork
scratching goblin ears might have
been frightening for a veggy, but i still
think they helped **leia** love me like a twit

and now she and i are close
while me and you are split;
but meg and julian help us
all connect
             and the
distance is only geography -

shit, i didn't realise i'd have
a zoom call relationship
with you, when you are
this young
             bit bored of
lockdown i suppose -
i miss you son.

                              dank

    it is dank - the shell of it,
    and if you peel it back then it is danker still.
    dank can mean resting - growing in the dark and wet -
    dank can mean ill.

    all the wonderings are this. full of promise;
    full of death; fit to burst; then nothing left -

    it swells the chest, then gone's the breath
    and nothing changes much
    nor ever will.

wall

clamour of advice givers
advise giving like a wall.
used to be that older folk
dropped the odd pearl -
the more uncertainty there is
the more the wall calls;
don't forget the bliss
of knowing nothing at all

ps

you are the hero
and i am afraid.
you are big
and i am small.
what is the point of taking issue?

doubt is lonely.
i will write my doubt down
in case someone understands

but also - without a bit more of it
we will sink this ship.

imposter

i feel like an imposter
tapping on the door
saying let me in

you ought to know
i have the wine dark sea
beneath my skin

now you're under there
trying to help
the phosphorescence win

i hope that you can swim
as well as i can
sit in dirt and sing

truth

the poet believes
both truths at once
the wise man
keeps one secret

you can live for love
or live by the gun
or do both
you fuckin eejut

borne

the baby wriggles feet and toes,
and hands and fingers next to those,
and legs and arms - the body grows,
crawls and clambers, climbs and rolls

early on this body dances;
early on it yearns to fly;
it feels a rhythm steady building
in laughter, and the tears it cries

it feels the need to reach out further

his chubby boyhood thighs
develop muscular as he grows older;
balletic flesh now, firm and slender -

movement builds, and movement dies
from daily dance school into slumber,
rising up and growing stronger;
shaping motion like a man now;
bridging chasms in his stride
- but striding's not enough - is dancing?

a dancer fully grown, he glides;
he dots his toes; he slides and lifts;
his teachers find in him a gift;
the truth is though, he hopes
a shift may come about, and one
mankind thus far has missed.

endeavours he - to soft, let go -
to build his strength to leap
and never-land;

he wants the fairy dust,
the air, and not the earth and sand;
he knew from when a child he must
take to the air and not come down.

he wants to fly - he wants to fly -
to king of skies be crowned -

....

years pass - he's in the theatre grand -

he never ceases practice,
an agility that's matchless,
makes mockery of the stage
that great black canvas.

all who see him watch and wonder
have there before been leaps like this?
some things are hid from audience members -
an unloved child, now narcissist;
they cannot see the pain, the desperate
wants and needs that shape their bliss -

he's driven by a frightening fervour;
the heights he gains - great airborne twists -
stem from frustration never shaken
that earth must call him for a kiss.

gravity cannot be beaten.
he cannot have his greatest wish.
he only aims for flight, for freedom,
but it's freedom that he misses.

. . . .

she sells tickets at the theatre door.
he daily passes her - she doesn't exist.
when she sees him her heart soars.
he wants more than she can ever give.

here she is - a woman like this.
caring as a caring person's
christmas present list;
open as an open fist;
quick as a comedian
yet quiet as closed lips;
eyes light green like lichen -
they see sadness in his hips

- when he walks so often by her;
one day he drops his script,
and before he has his hands on it
she gives him what she's picked up.

" - sorry - "
"no, that's alright."
" - well - good day... miss - "

she caught his eye. something stirs in him.
he denies it - but it insists.

her hair is wild as the woodland;
he aims for the stars above;
he does not know how he'll get there;
he fights, but he falls in love.

the moment of fall is certain.
it's an evening performance in autumn -

she's at the back of the auditorium
- he sees her as he walks on
stage from the dark of the wings
and he can't help that his heart sings.

. . . .

he dances but the dance is different
for love is the glue that binds all things
and now it bonds his moves with rhythm,
the rhythm that love brings -

it's felt in the waves as they land on the shore
and the leaves that spin in the winds;
it's felt in the soil as it's turned by a fork
and the heat of the sun on the skin -

the audience sense that something's changed;
his need for the heights doesn't win -

he dances not for the spectacle,
not for the elegant sight of him,
not to escape, not to be king,
not to jump up and away from everything -

he can feel wings beating in his heart's chambers
and makes no leap, builds to no flourish;
his feet caress the floor, yet never more
has he been flying; he is nothing, graceful, shining;

the want in which he's caged himself,
locked by his pride, is dying - but

- now there's something changed again.
this is a dance in which love reigns;
love is change, and change is pain;
his dance starts stuttering, half-deranged -

if you've spent your life alone
can you suddenly be saved?

his hands begin to green and darken;
his face falls grave; she watches as his fingers
crack apart and harden: something's happening -
something's wrong. "please," she says,
"please give him pardon."

but whose help can she ask?

the saviour is love's transformation:

she watches as his hand's break apart -

wooden-coloured paintbrush bristles burst
through his fingers like thistles through soil;
she cannot help him; his dancing quickens;
impossibly fast, then through thick oil; he is a human
marionette - with body, arms and legs, and feet
and head - and yet it seems his mind's possessed;
the dancing strangely glorious; he's slicked in sweat
and - "look!" - he's horse-hair edged; now bereft
of hands, with nowhere to hide, his mouth gaping wide,
paint pours from the wrists where two brushes arrived.

a glob of white lands. then the red of the damned.
the green of the woods - the yellow of best made plans
- the hot pink of plans smashed and made new;
he splashes a story lustrous and true; slashed, stroked
and spilled; dolloped orange and blue - he faints
and then wakes; and then screams as he paints;
this dance is so old that the whole theatre shakes;
nothing seen like this since matter was sewn;
the light he now makes on the stage is a home;
it's a place where a universe new can be grown;
for loving can change a man more than he knows.

crumbling, breaking, he draws to a close -
his feet cease to flex; there is death in his toes
- the black stage more colourful than summer meadows
and he falls into the mess of it nose deep,
then over he goes to corpse pose -

the brushes for hands swivel, spit and then slow
as he exhales his last - yes, his final breath goes.

"no - " she whispers - she's winded as though hit;
been through all of it; felt his every whip of pain,
but she's strong as woman is; she steps across to sit
beside his lifeless body; his pale face; his blue lips.

the paint is wet - and moving; this is a tapestry that shifts;
the fibres twine and fit together close as knit on winter mitts;
a kaleidoscopic snake pit; the creation of a fit;
a smash of sewing kit -

the spectators in the theatre stunned -
a tourist screams; "what the hell is this?!"
from stage she calls; "is there a doctor in the house...?"
- but now the stage begins to lift...

he has danced a magic carpet.
he has given her a gift.
a dance unto his death.
"please," she begs, "not this - "

she leans - if only for one kiss to share with him.
she sighs a sigh... he breathes it in -
a gasp into the well of him.
a gasp that says love wins.

his hands are back; he holds hers in;
the magic carpet ripples with love's rhythm -

and now nothing is amiss. the very roof compromises,
by opening - just a bit. the audience clap. a lot.
wait. that's not the end of this. they kiss.
and don't stop kissing - then they fly to where they wish -

leaves

the evening sun refreshes the mood
of autumn about to turn winter,
like ginger beer after oxtail, rice and peas
refreshes the throat of the drinker.

"sink a long draught of me - "
says the sun to the leaves on the trees,
"before you say goodbye
and float a little on the breeze - "

through

belly

- a haar!!!!!

pirates shouting! sounding like a caricature!

but they were not - they were boarding
and at swording we were amateur.
captain from the ship went falling;
they went calling out for more;
our boat was filled with treasure troves,
and our sickness was the law -

- a haar!!!!!

those dirty wastrels cried,
gums dark from naught but bread;
the lack of lemon and lime to eat
had lost light from their heads;
so they boarded us, those vagabonds
with eyes on jewels in cabins,
as we protected treasure troves
and they fled from their famine.

we sang a song to bwoy us up,
but sang it silently
because we had what'er we wanted
- aah, our hearts went quietly

we held our swords aloft
and our invaders went

- a haar!!!

we knew we were for davy jones's
locker down in dark -

they slaughtered many - most of us -
they made our treasure theirs;
they kept me - only me - alive
as i had learned to stare

they didn't like our pretty boat
so slow when theirs was fast -
they nailed me on it, nearly dead;
not bow - on boom, near mast -

now head to wind they kept me there
whilst feasting of their spoils -
and as my sunned skin hardened in
they massaged me with oils -

they cut me through from balls to neck;
made spillage of me on the deck -
they shouted - haar!! - and i gulped - heck...
they stuffed gold doubloons in my neck
and as i swung above the deck they shouted all

- a haar!

our boat, new theirs, was heavy
and it could not ride low tide;

it often stuck on silted bed
for many nights to lie
and wait unwelcome guests
to come and make its burden light.

their boat had neither treasure,
nor took many planks to make;
they only knew the ocean's codes
and that they needed take.

their boat went fast and ours went slow;
they liked theirs better - this i know -
i watched them let their belly grow;
they swapped the winds for monied sloth -

you take until you take too much,
then let the takers in -
slipped is the guard as belly fills
and in comes wandering
another shark with belly dark,
no bread to find within -
from mast to bow they moved me
figure-dead of what had been,
yet i was freshly gutted -
they were fat, and i now thin.

they sailed off down the river,
the new captain whistling a note,
as a dead me felt the bottom jolt
against that heavy laden boat.

eating tomatoes

in slovenia they ask me:
is it really true in england
they have signs that say - 'private'?

the son laughs - "get off my land!!!"
have another homemade brandy says the dad.
they shake their heads and chuckle,
as if such a thing could be possible.

i hold my head in my hands
thinking of families forced out of flats
and barbed wire fences round gardens.

their neighbour's name is marian.
same as robin hood's missus i tell him.
try my tomatoes he demands.

dart

she's like a golden dart of honey.
she's all i need. she pleases me
like flowers in summer and like the bumblebees.
when i grasp onto nothing she guides in me release -
sometimes i search for oceans parting,
the waves to fall on me; i hear her under,
strumming heart strings, deep beneath the seas
and go to her; her eyes are lark's wings,
her teeth piano keys; she holds me
like i'm precious while i root her like a tree
and when the waves tear at my leaves
she speaks kind to the breeze that eases;
unto it we're borne, together to be free -
we fly and dive the seas and skies
and grant us both safety; when parted
we are half alive; together, wise as unity.

war

for how many
must it have been the last thing
   "mummy"

heart rending when
my son says it in the shower
with soap in his eye
   "i want my mummy"

for how many
must it have been the last thing
   "mummy"
      "i want my mummy"
last thing before they die

house-sitting

it is really too cold
i have not enough clothes
as i sit in the flesh
of a house that is old
perhaps it has skin
perhaps i can sew
a rhyme that holds warmth
round a fire made of soul

dark

someone says; how do i bear
the weight of the dark at four?
when winter comes a-knocking
bringing darkness to my door?

someone else says; i can bear it
since my son's killer was caught.
another says a quarantini
tends to settle thought.

i say; i like to walk in it -
it's what it's for - to walk
and swim and walk some more
- and when my face is under
the soft onslaught of nothing
let pause effect and cause.

the dark is for the senses
that are more given a miss;
it comes close and wraps
around you if you let its
blackness kiss - the dark is
without laws: how do you bear
the weight of the dark at four?

open up the door and let it pour
- it can touch you on your edges,
it can nestle in your core, and
though some things may sound
through it, it never deigns to talk;

and strange enough the truth is
- when it's light that you have sought -
the weight of dark is lighter; with light
there's something there to court,
but the dark is gentle absence
and in absence comes reward:
you can sense your soul in darkness,
though not if you're in thought.

the dark's the space that grows
the beauty; the centre of the seed
that grows the tree, oak yet to be,
resting quietly in the middle of acorns -
you'll find there blissful nothing's taught;
but if you do not match the nothing?
to your flaws dark holds a torch.

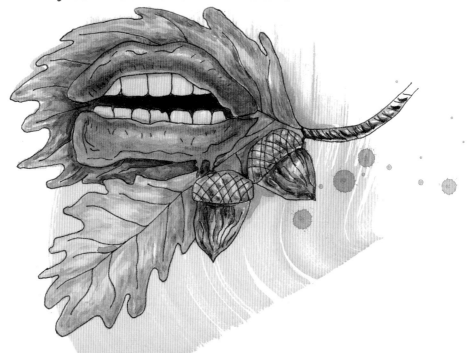

                    come

    in the cemetery at the end of the road
    come spring time the flowers grow
    like migrating birds taking flight -
    launching to new life

    sudden as a loved wife
    coming on her wedding night
    in olden days and other climes
    when that first time tight parts first tie

    what i'm saying is
    - the flowers are a surprise;
    not, of course, to those who lie below
    and give the colours height

    i love them those dead people
    for rotting down so bright;
    o let them rot this winter
    that spring will come so light

                    fungi

it's true the oak and the cypress
      grow not in eachother's shadow
but did you know
                beneath the soil
  between enormities of tree
that equal those above
delicate and slow the fungi stretches?

subtle, microscopic, soft suggestions
  of caresses
            a toil of no's and yes's
coil roots - in silence interconnected
    unity courses
                whilst the oak thinks not
of being oak, the cypress not
            of being green

                            they stand
in the light
            touching quiet in the dark,
and the winds rustle both of their leaves.

'donkey song'
for liam's dad

can you hear the donkeys call
sharp notes and horns?
life and what's beyond
of ee's and or's
before's and after's?

from a fence top
beside the pastures
pavarotti on little speakers
turns fur-filled ears

bend your ear closer
to find notes as gentle
as a blossom's tumble
on spring breeze -

it's not the tenor mpthree'd
by rough old hands
round new technologies

- hear harmonies between the brays;
a sing-along of noble carriers accompanies

with heaven high notes
and then the ground grass
wet between their teeth

to think of you,
how steadily you took your fill;

you heel-toed your boots
across life beautifully.

you slung the load
and led the way
to hayricks stuffed
for winter days

with strength enough
to shoulder children's
cries away, and men
and women's too

sometimes we all are weak
and always love will do;
it can be seen in tender eyes
and the hard tread of a hoof

love can be seen when nothing's said
as there's more work to do;
love can be seen when nothing's said
as there's no need between two.

the donkeys carry strong their weight
- they whisper, i love you

they close dark eyes
to night from light
or light from night
who knows what might -

bye dad, enjoy the view

crown-wearing

for the parasitic people cull corona comes.
can we lose the old, and then some young?
my dad says; son, we'd both be gone;
but i don't want her on her own - your mother -

so we scrabble humans, heavy hearts;
fitting truth to fear lumps, fight to be together
- money swabbed plastic in ocean noses;
"she's better at this now that nurse is - "

pulled apart. one man sits alone in dark.
two lovers flourish. two find fists hard.
slow learning to let go; working for a way to
wear the crown well; sifting endings for a start.

pandemusing

i know it is not a war
about which we shall not speak,
but i question whether can we?
the suffering is very deep
but subtle like a handmaid's
tale that slow unfolds with
feelings that cannot be shown --
o my old friend i wish you know
that which you know already;
once we could pick up the phone;
now fear that catching up is heavy
has drawn a distance we must wait
to bridge; please know i think
of you, and that i miss you very.

loving

understanding why or how
to love yourself can seem
silly but is simple.

love is in action.

you are not expected to
feel good about yourself:
just to do something
so that you feel good.

oh, and check in that
it really does make you feel good.
you'll know because you love yourself.

weird me

you can't be abandoned
if you are on your own.
you can't be made homeless
if you don't have a home.
you can't be un-loved
if you love no-one else;
run, he says; run -
you are best by yourself -

but i love and am loved;
we're warm under our roof -
but he'll come, the weird me
who knows he's the truth.
weird me who will come
and he's only the fear
of a child, just a boy
whose family's not near,
who grew up an addict
so he could stay clear
of the chance to be loved
for loved ones disappear.

weird me doesn't love me,
i wish that he'd stay
outside of my head
somewhere far far away;
he thinks that he loves me;
he knows, really knows
that me and him function
much better alone -

he says we're the best —
that we're better than you;
he's afraid if he loves you
you won't love him too —

though he'll ask you to love him
and shine like the moon
but without as much substance;
the shine's built on gloom —

i've decided to love him;
we'll be one and not two,
like the world is, for union
is what love can do.
i don't want to be split;
i want to be true
to the best side of me —

what's the worst that
the weird me can do?

well he can destroy me
if i don't watch him closely
and thank him so gently
for trying to help me —

come under my wing, me
— i have your back too
but i'm a grown up, me
— i've worked to see truly;
and you're still a child, me
— so i'll look after you.

                    chapel
          for joan and michalis

if of an eve you chance
to climb into a chapel
between two houses
you may find a candle lit for all;
you may lie down.
                    a deep below
will strum your soul; it will,
don't think about; settle soft
above the cut beneath;
the ocean throbs there deep;
you hear it loud
                    and from you springs
knowledge people chase
the speed they run from djinns
- you came for pardon from yourself
asking why you cannot sing - "who is he?"
you have asked; "who is the one
i can call king?"
                    you know that you
know little, as you reach for everything;
just that each day is the end of it
and each day it begins.
you wish to find?
                    so question -
then lean back into the winds and listen.
you can hear the cavern if you're still.
rest on your wings. there's comfort
in the centre of you, love,
and of all things.

                    90

eyelashes

    i had a dream between
a man with a great nose
(nostrils that could gather worlds)
and a girl with eyelashes
that scattered gold.
    he was old and she was young,
and so the story goes:
she pressed his forehead on her thumb
and his eye there cracked from closed.
    monstrous excellent it saw,
this new-found aperture,
through many doors
that opened with it.
    he rose and strode
from that strange fold
that had seemed to shape,
case-like, his soul.
    the god-he found it bright,
a touch unwieldy -
for he could both destroy with zest
and could create sincerely.
    his hands were fission tearing cannons
that caressed leaves from buds;
his toes were knarled and long
and in between them there bled mud.
    his dark eye did not blink
as he began to carve anew
and when it closed, as he was done,
again all he was still.

rhythm

the bud opens
time passes
watch for the moments
the grace of the unfurl
the light of life
pregnant moments
moments of fall
gradual growth
standing tall
the wind blows
and there is
nothing left at all
through all these moments
there is one thing if you listen
all things pass but love
love links the moments
love has rhythm

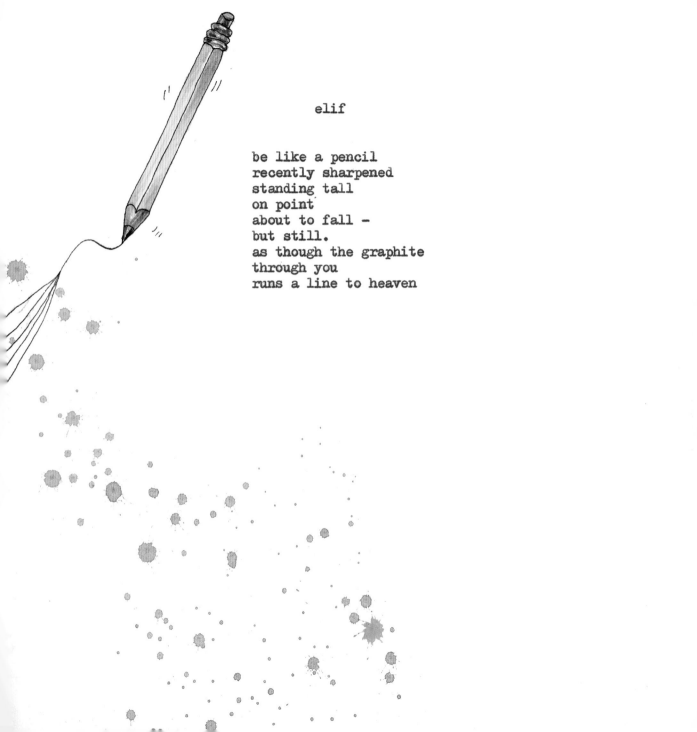

elif

be like a pencil
recently sharpened
standing tall
on point
about to fall –
but still.
as though the graphite
through you
runs a line to heaven

ruby
for mum and dad

forty years of bliss - well, let's be realistic -
it can be hit and miss this long-haul romance business...

sometimes kisses soft as peaches
sometimes words as hard as fists
and the reaches of the effortful
are never much but through a mist
that parts as often as a risk is taken

risks of heart, to bring the sight, to bring the gift -
for a simple palette's good, but another's colours lift,
though not always easy welcomed - colours startle and they kick;
red ruby cut 'mongst jungle leaves can tear and it can rip;
it can blood the dirt it grows in - the patient pick up all the bits
to build a picture back more clear, to find a rhythm that in both fits:
quarry man, quarry woman, quarry nature, hells and heavens;
dive in again, be brave, be brave, dive in again with lips;
dive in like movie lovers and dive in like clumsy twits -
scorn the lover, then admire them, eat the fruit and spit the pips;
grow the forest - burn it down - for life goes round;
does it go upwards or go down? it all passes -
passes easier when we hold our hands together,
grit our teeth and leap into the nothing of forever
with a smile and not a frown; to work for love is an endeavour;
it's a parcel marked to share; can be heavy as an elly;
can be lighter than a feather - can you hold up in the air
a white elephant presented by a meanie maharaja,
full of majesty and promise, always breaking from the tether?

perhaps you are a warrior? a high-risk love investor?
then the love may grow some stronger. strong enough to let go?
to surrender? what if the elephant's a stomper?
a wild and heavy danger...

                              o! - if elephants might fly -
they can.

elegant elephant
wedding white
uncertain future
a little needy
a little shaky
uncertainty
propped by beauty;
must untie the legs
then strengthen -
cut the leather
cut the linen;
prop the wood
and iron in;
soon come tin
- reinforcing
with some steel -
now this elephant
is looking like
she's supported
by love's feeling -
on her fourteenth anniversary
don't give her any ivory
no jewellery, nor gold -

just cuddle her big belly;
within this elly cultivate
a true love nursery
with growing certainty
that she will gain more colours –
first of rainbow glazéd china;
sparkling silver; subtle pearl;
coral red, then red as ruby;
if you love the beastie truly
it is whispered wings are sprouting
slowly for a trunking outing –

that is to say that love 'tween two sails elephants up high
which is everso commendable because, for recreational,
rainbow love-elephants trunk-trumpet true love from the skies

so you should know, yous twos who try love, fail love –
and then again begin to try – you can raise aloft and rain love
trumpeted from eletrunks trunking true love far and wide;

and we have you, who try, to thank – thanks mum and dad
for lightening love's weight, through all those bloody hells
and bloody whys, and all the search for bloody honesty and
all the phosphorescent sighs – for it is good (and some say wise)
to sail an elephant up high: they might surprise a passerby
with a little eletrumpeting of two's perseverant love combined.

seal

we see ourselves
through the eyes of others
but we can make new laws
starting with our own truth
time over, and again.

when my old mate seal
finished that time in the pen
my shave had become hair
and i was studying shakespeare.

seal's loud across
the squat in shoreditch;
"goodbye!" he hollers
(he means hello - goodbye
is my name at the time)
"i hear you're a thespian
now bruv! wicked!!!"
he says it with the
glimmer of a smile.

seal's a serious guy.
holds every weight lifting
record in that brick pile nick;
gets up off the shower room
floor to earn with fists
the name 'the don'
when they give him the shiv.

when i draw small poems
next to sketched illustrations
with the odd suggestion of how
to brave the test, and old mates
check in to say; "it's different bruv -
but yes - " it feels excellent.

if your now is not working,
whoever you're surrounded by,
whatever your self-expectations,
you can re-invent.

maybe you have to fight,
start fresh, or run for miles.
part of you will face death.
let it die. then give yourself
your seal of approval.
get up off the tiles.

a body

inside a body there's a tremor;
it can be very small.
it rests in flesh that's gripping
tight because we fall.

inside a body there's a world
that can't call out; that hides;
that stalls; that wears a mask -
that isn't us, yet is us all.

there can be sorrow hid around
a heart since we were small.

our bodies are alive with these full
stories that we've soaked in.
there, beneath your skin -

can you feel the tension stretching?
shoulder wings in straps of sinew;
wraps of living; clinging; sheets of feeling;
can you feel your body dancing?

can you feel the promises you never made,
or kept? the words unspoken in your neck?
the hopes heart-held inside your chest?

the efforts in your diaphragm?
those made, and when you did not

brave the test - and when sometimes,
on occasion, yes, it was effortless -

can you feel love, and love repressed,
coiled tight inside the many parts of body
curling round that bowl of bone above your legs?

we are majesty, and we are less.
we are filled with darkness,
except where spheres of light
shine bright inside our heads -

orbs swift become instruction
carried through the dark and wet

we are many, and we are kept
in muscle; in myofascial webs;
a body holds itself together;
scaffolded in vertebrae; in jaw
bones - in our compressed layers;
the sorrow; the joy; the stress, so -

forgive. forget. sit and rest.
be kind and take a breath, and it will pass -

through galaxies
disguised as cells,
through pipes of life
that will be dead

through everything we wish to be
and know not that we wish to be
and can't let go, and then can let;

our many lives are body sized,
a perfect tapestry of flesh -
a bloody mess - how does it feel?
me too. i confess.

our lungs are full this moment,
and now there's nothing left.

what is success? i don't know.
what happens when i let go
all the way, before i flex?
is the wind passing my skin?
is it mixing with my breath?
is the paper thin? the ink?
the more i sense the less i think.
the less i think the less i guess.

each second is different -
not good, better, or best.
i can see and i can feel
the wooden of my desk;
the moon's light as it reflects;
beyond my window -
there's a wall;
in it more windows;
a neighbour stands
there in a vest.

the light is high,
the moon arrives,
the dog steals socks,
the room's a mess -

i am new now like a baby;
old as cause and then effect;
and i know that i am with you
because everything connects.

This book is based on a true story. In certain cases, incidents, characters, names and timelines have been changed, and are products of poetic license and the author's imagination.

Our deep gratitude to those below for your encouragement,
time, care, effort, skillsets, and support of this book,
and of all the other art that stems from these poems.
It is in wide-hearted unity and community that we make
the world a better place. Thank you so much.

Marie Segger, James Fransham, Ben Kenward, Bota Zakir,
Joelle Taylor, Jacob Proud, Matthew Reilly, Sheree Reilly,
Jane Glennie, Scott Lavene, Simon Lohmeyer, Mario Voit,
Phoebe Ihenacho, Heidi Ihenacho, Zinah Ihenacho,
Amechi Ihenacho, Chris Hammond, Pixie Lisette Lawrie,
Bridget Kenward, Robert Kenward, Lawrence Alexander,
Nidhal Schlanz, Karl Schlanz, John Tynan, Jack Blackburn,
Meghan Lambert, Julian Wilson, Stephen Myth, Sara Peyron,
Theo Griffiths, Hedvig Weibull, Gerrit Machetanz, 1tee,
Remy Dietze, Yamin Choudury, Becca Thomason, Othman Read,
Juan Diego Saldaño, Zeus, Alfonso Fernández Sanchez,
Emma Luffingham, Alessandra McAllister, Molly Dixon,
Peter Hansen, Christian Pfeiffer, Subtry, Gabriel Xavier,
Pav4n, Alexander Hubmann, Kitty Bishop, Jan Krause,
Niti Acharya, Oliver Dorrell, Liam Buckley, Marc Hacker,
Matt Harlock, Tobias Kapteinet, Joe Davey, James Frostick,
Sarah Henley Bennett, Caroline Bennett, Johnny Shanahan
and Brandon Lee Henry.

James E. Kenward wrote and performed lyric-based sketches
for the BBC's Sony Academy Award-nominated show 'A Series of
Psychotic Episodes'. James wrote and played the lead role, an
emcee and poetic narrator, for 'Streets - A New Kind of Musical',
which was reprised for several runs on the London stages.
As a vocalist for jungle drum and bass music, James worked
internationally with many legends of the club and rave scene.

When James is not writing or performing poetry he works
in clinical and private practice as a massage therapist.
His career in the medical field informs his writing.

This is James's debut poetry collection.

Leia Lorelai has a BSc in psychology, and an MSc in
mindfulness and neuroscience from King's College London.
Leia works as a yoga teacher. At the time of publication
she is in her final years of medical studies, consolidating
her understanding of health and the bodyself so as to most
effectively combine modern science with ancient wisdom.

This is Leia's first collection of illustrations.